Castor Oil Uses, Magic and Benefits

PTR **LMDumizulu**

Dearest...

Is it factual that certain plants have tremendous natural magical powers?
The Clear answer is Yes indeed.
The magic is in the smoke, normally called incense (*chaunga/ impepho/qhumiso*) the smell, shape (*intambo yokuqhumisela*), season and at times the process and occasion.
There is a tree I know in Afrika.
If you collect its dried twigs, leaves, cut off logs for firewood or build a kraal pen, a house or granary, even the most loving family will be disrupted. If you get in touch, I will give you the name.
There is also a bird whose furthers create havoc.
I know a young man who doubted this. So, one day he caught that bird pulled a few feathers and attended a white wedding. The pastor spent half the day casting out Satan and demons to no avail. Eventually there was serious anarchy and pandemonium. The wedding flopped.

Here are Some Bantu names for Castor oil Plant~ *Pfuta, Futa, MuPfuta.*

Castor Oil Plant -Scientific Name; RICINUS COMMUNIS.

Please Read this before you proceed.

MuPfuta has 2 Major benefits.
 (i) the popular *physical benefits* and the,
 (ii) not so popular darker *spiritual* uses.

We will share with you very significant Spiritual aspects first in Section 1. Then in Section 2 we suggest some sources to explore on the physical benefits of castor oil.

Some critical themes.

How did Afrikans -Bantus on earth know about these plants?
It is true that they were unknown to the Africans at first.
Therefore, our ancestors must have either used INTUITION, experimentation or keen observation to access such knowledge.
Secondly, they may have received this knowledge via *revelation* through an Ancestor, Netcher, Creation Laws or The Creator. This maybe the major reason we find many African sages who attained 'godlike' or divine magical status in ancient times?

.... We read in an ancient Papyri the following…
"...to me belonged the universe before you gods had come into being. You have come afterwards because I am Heka."
                Coffin texts, spell 261 First Intermediate Period to Middle Kingdom

PLEASE READ OUR Disclaimer.

PTR LMDumizulu shall in no way be held responsible by any Legal, Moral, Direct or Indirect means for the abuse of this MuPfuta Ritual... This booklet shall not be used as a substitute for your official and licensed consultation or remedy.

The results of many others should not be the basis to measure the efficacy of this system but Our "African" Oral and Written Ancestral Testimony. Ancestral Taboos demand that the user must employ this plants' or any of its by-products *for healing, defense, psychic boost and demoniacal protection.*

Consequently, you may not consume, inhale directly, smoke or other ways nor use it for revenge attacks or any other way that is intended to bring about injury, spiritual damage or physical harm to self or others....

Information revealed herein is for educational purposes and spiritual understanding.

This work may not be reproduced taught or shared without a verbal agreement from the Healer.

Section 1.
Spiritual Detoxing.

What is heka?
Do You Need to KNOW THIS?

So called **Black Science** always involved Magic. The misunderstanding of the word magic is quite recent. However, it is what our ancestors in Egypt termed Haka. The *Greeks* and modern Egyptologist say **Heka**. *Haka* is a ChiKaranga Bantu word denoting connecting to another realm... or to something, just like the English term *hook*! Some traditional healers hook your illness to themselves and burn it off. They can also exorcise spirits using Kuhaka too. In an esoteric sense it is that which is known as Ukuhlakanipha/ wisdom. **Magic fascinated people. Even today Miracles baffles and creates extraordinary scenes in religion and life.**

Modern Magic Episodes
A smartphone will bamboozle those who lived 800 years ago!
In their eyes it is MAGIC! Why does magic appeal to the masses? Because it was and is practical and appears to directly violate the natural laws.
The Impossible becomes an option. Consider the popular *flying* basket vehicle technology.

Flying in Baskets

We know some tribesmen who work in faraway countries, many kilometers away. For example, they live with their families in say Malawi. But they commute daily to Johannesburg, finish work maybe around 17.30 hrs. and knock off. They then fly to Malawi in their basket vehicle. *See diagram below*. The operating principles of this flying machine are hidden from the ordinary people, but revealed to the knowledgeable. Its magic so too with the following ritual.

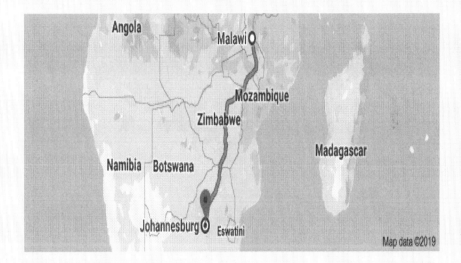

Magical Power and Demon Casting Ritual

The Castor Oil plant was once found only in Africa?
Do You Know this was once a Celebrated tree on earth?

Then it spread into the far east and some scholars now say it is a native Indian plant! Many of the species are genetically modified and have been commercialized. Thus, rendering them powerless spiritually.

Summary of uses and benefits.
Mu **Pfuta has many uses. It has ONE Powerful spiritual use that has eluded millions. We shall give you the ritual shortly.**
 The magical benefits of Castor oil are legendary.
 In ancient Rome they called it **Palma Christi**, rendered today as the healing hand of Jesus Christ. Again, there are reasons why.
From an ancient papyrus found in Africa we are aware that this plant, specifically its seeds can be used to heal the *lymphatic system, restart hair growth, massage, removing skin moles and warts, useful in cancer therapy, therapeutic cure of knees and breast pains* and many other conditions.

It is the only Plants whose beans destroy Anthrax!

As indicated above it has a spiritual use which is almost not elaborated by many scholars,' researchers and healers.

Warning:
THIS IS A DEADLY Plant!

The hull of Pfuta Seeds contains a deadly poison called **ricin**.
Thus, **in that sense it is a very deadly plant if used unwisely.**
The *Ricinus communis* (Castor Oil Plant) is a species of plant in the family Euphorbiaceous. It is *a **photoautotrophic*** plant, meaning that during its life it generates its food from abiotic sources and captures energy from light. This is vital to know. Since we also intend to share its magical characteristics.

From the website https://emergency.cdc.gov/agent/ricin/facts.asp, we Learn more about this poison. Ricin is-

- a poison found naturally in castor beans. If castor beans are chewed and swallowed, the released ricin can cause injury. Ricin can be made from the waste material left over from processing castor beans.
- It can be in the form of a powder, a mist, or a pellet, or it can be dissolved in water or weak acid.
- It is a stable substance under normal conditions, but can be inactivated by heat above 80 degrees centigrade (176 degrees Fahrenheit).

Spirit is Power Release.
the Magic of Castor Oil Beans...

Caution... The seeds you are using must be genuine not GMOS or hybrids. Think and Visualize the results you are aiming for before you engage in this ritual.

Your critical step is to Define your Intention or goals Plainly.

Write it in a few words. You may ask yourself, *"why am i desiring to Burn Pfuta Incense?"*

Your Answer maybe *driving out uninvited spirits/negative vibes.*

But Be specific ...
what is the name of the spirit you want out?
if you know or suspect someone is playing games (spiritually) even by way of negative thoughts MuPfuta incense will work, **ON CONDITION-** *you are not the agent provocateur. (You Have not provoked or attacked first!)*
Name the effects of this negative spirit or vibe.
What is it doing to you, your family or loved ones...?
That is YOUR Proof i.e. causing depressions, despondence or other illnesses... This is the most powerful ingredient used to free you from ANY demons, Evil spirit Or Satan Himself or Herself when using... This Pfuta plant...

Process.

Some Critical House Keeping.

Next is self-introspection.

Clean your conscience first.

If you know some issues that are within your soul, actions that you have done and are knowingly against Ma'at/Ubuntu... i.e. slept with neighbor's wife etc... Clear that baggage first...

Why ... Because that event creates a counter wave that will negative your spiritual vortex around which other negatives may slide through during the rituals. Your lock and key here are YOUR Actions, attitude, INTENT and Goals. NO ONE should go scotch free for attacking the innocent!

So, if you are "germ-free", spiritually innocent and morally feel you are being attacked for Unknown aberrations, proceed without hesitation. This is an all-purpose ritual that is completed after the usual UBUNTU/Isintu/Unhu confessions.

Make Sure you use African seeds. At Least that way we Know we are in the ancestral footpath.

Process

Select perhaps 4 or 5 Pfuta seeds.

Put them in your Palms.

Activate them by breathing on them and shake them a little. As You do so thank The Creator for giving us this plant to use for our benefit. And Our wise Ancestors for discovering it many uses. Give them Praise and thanks.

In your Vernacular!

Crush or Grind them into Fine Paste.

Do not add anything.

Other rituals may differ depending on the intent Others teach that you may mix them with ram fat, some herbal oils or other herbs but we insist that for this initial ritual use Pfuta alone.

You may put the Paste in a sealed container, brown or khaki envelope or tradition non-metal non-plastic container...this is temporary.

Tools.

You need a ritualized incense burner.

It must have a solid handle. Not the swinging handle.

A Clay incense burner is the best though you may use stone or wood*,

NO Metal, Plastic, ceramic or Humidifies...

The color must be Black or Brown.

Shape

Roundish, Cylindrical- Not square...

The Problem to Surmount.

If You live in AFRIka its easy.

You will have to Select your incense fire from clean trees or firewood.

However, in other continents this may be an issue. Because you need to know the clean and unclean trees. Firewood must be from clean TREES! You must be aware that certain trees are deemed Unclean. Even amongst indigenous trees. Worse off those that were planted in Africa by colonizers and enslavers. Therefore, the best would be coke or charcoal. The one you use for your barbecue may be the best option.

This Ritual Must be PERFORMED at Night Not Midnight, Morning or Noon.

DO NOT Inhale THE Smoke!

Put a few red ambers, hot coals into your incense burner.

Sprinkle a few Pfuta Paste into the hot ashes to create minimal smoke/Incense.

HERE IS THE Key.

Make Sure YOUR first step is started with your LEFT foot.

The Burner should be in your Left hand too! This makes it a Left-hand Ritual externally but since the declaration of your intent is for good use you Your Heart is in it. The negative spiritual force you are generating will be the force to correct your situation.

IF IN DOUBT STOP.

Left foot forward.

As You walk around your home or room swing your burner in all directions east then west, upward and downward, south and then north... Be carefully.

Whisper your demands with authority.

USE an AFRICAN language.

After this some usually leave the burner outside or near their doors. But we suggest you extinguish the fire. Restore the Burner into a neutral state.

See ** Below...

Remove the clothes you were wearing and put them separately from the rest...

Wash as usual and have an excellent Night But

Oh, One more thing Left...

**Please Note.

DO NOT share this information with anyone.

We left everything to your GOOD intentions.

This is an ancestral ritual and has a spiritual signature.

After the ritual throw away extra Castor Bean powder wash the burner with Spring water. Put the burner upside down in your Alter.

OUR Ancestors believed that the oil was an effective treatment for treating diseases caused by demons. Is it true that every African has a demon? *"Farewell (bis) Anobvisa, the good ox-herd, Anobvisa (bis), the son of a (?) jackal (and?) a dog . . . another volume saith: the child of . . . Isis (?) (and) a dog, Nabrishoth, the Cherub (?) of Amenti, king of those of.....' Say seven times.*

https://www.gutenberg.org/files/43662/43662-h/43662-h.htm
https://www.scribd.com/document/208380229/The-Key-to-All-Sacred-Mysteries-Lies-in-Ancient-Egypt

NOTICE

IF You do this ritual count 21 days. Observe your dreams, record any unusual encounters or life events. If you feel we need to know please email us ... Otherwise we are excited to share this.

Any Questions Do Not Hesitate get in Touch ...

Section 2;

Applied Knowledge.

Ancient Afrikans practised a credible form of medicine 1,900 years before Galen. Christian pastors, evangelists and prophets ridicule African traditional healers or spiritual aspects of Bantu culture. They call natural healers as Witchdoctors, demons or Satan's servants. Incidentally in emergency situations they are quick to call an ambulance or swallow some tablets, pills or rub Vicks, go to hospital or visit doctor, gets an injection pop a pill. They must realise they have just been healed by the same system started by AFRIKAN Witchdoctors and copied by the Greeks!

Of late modern medicine has verified the materia medica and efficacy of prescriptions recorded from the time of **Amenemhet III** (1842–1797 BC) to **Ramses III** (1182–1151 BC), a period pivotal to the history of pharmacy. The oldest and clear medical documents were discovered in Afrika. One of them is known as the Ebers Papyrus. Named after the man who bought it.

KEY MEDICAL PAPYRI

- The Kahun (1825 B.C)
  -gynecology
- The Ebers (1534 B.C?)
  -internal medicine
- The Edwin Smith Surgical Papyrus (1600 B.C)
  -surgical wounds and fractures

The Ebers papyrus (top) and Edwin Smith Surgical Papyrus (bottom)

https://slideplayer.com/slide/7335453/

It is clear that our ancestors were well advanced in medicine.

They also used herbs to heal and engaged in demon casting too...

An example is the castor oil plant, as in several entries in the Ebers Papyrus: a) One crushes its roots in water, to place on a head which is sick: he will then become well immediately, like one who is not ill. b) A little of its fruit (beans) is chewed with beer by a man with wehi-condition in his faeces. This is an elimination of disease from the belly of a man.... d) Its oil (merhet) is also prepared from its fruit (beans) to anoint [a man] with wehau-skin disease.... which is painful.... Some remedies contained as many as thirty-seven items. It is unclear whether an item was an active principle, a vehicle, or simply added for taste. Honey, for example, might work for all three categories...

https://www.encyclopedia.com/science-and-technology/chemistry/organic-chemistry/castor-oil

Amenemhet 3

https://www.aldokkan.com/egypt/amenemhet3.htm

Other uses...

-Cancer Research.

It is also used in cancer treatment. We post a clinical extract below.

'An immunotoxin (IT) was prepared from monoclonal antibody (MoAb) 115D8 and ricin A chain. MoAb 115D8 is directed against the carcinoma-associated sialomucin MAM-6. In a protein synthesis inhibition assay this IT was cytotoxic for the human breast cancer cell line T47D.
https://www.researchgate.net/publication/20024610_Endocytosis_and_intracellular_routing_of_an_antibody-ricin_A_chain_conjugate

Castor Oil Used In Nylon Manufacturing.

Castor oil is also used in the production of sebacic acid, a vital constituent in the manufacture of nylon and other synthetic resins and fibers. Commercial use of Castor-Oil is popular in INDIA where it has been harnessed to boost manufacturing of many diverse products. READ more from the website quoted below.

http://whatsup-indianstockideas.blogspot.com/2014/02/jayant-agro-castor-oil-indian-institute.html

Castor Bean Oil has been used in machines due to its superior "oiliness" and ability to "cling" on friction prone hot moving components. Its used in racing cars and high-performance engines. It is the basic ingredient of Castrol-R racing motor oil for high speed automobile and motorcycle engines. Castor oil is a popular fuel additive for two cycle engines, and imparts a distinctive aroma to the exhaust of these engines. Castor wax, a hard wax produced by the hydrogenation (chemical combination with hydrogen) of pure castor oil, is used in polishes, electrical condensers, carbon paper, and as a solid lubricant. https://www.penriteoil.com.au/knowledge-centre/Castor-Oils/184/The-History-of-Castor-Oil/394#/

From the https://en.wikipedia.org/wiki/Castor_oil .

In World War I, castor bean oil was used in Allied rotary aircraft engines such as the Gnome monosoupape (on a rotary the engine case and cylinders spin around a fixed crankshaft) because of its superior lubricating qualities, and much to the dismay of the pilots of the time, also a powerful laxative. One can imagine what slang terms resulted from that item alone.

Around 1905, The Society of Automobile Engineers was formed in the USA and took on the task of setting the standards for engine oil. They made the decision to compare and define lubricating oils by viscosity. Viscosity, in layman's terms, is how easily a liquid pour.

The SAE decided to compare the viscosity of oils at 100 degrees centigrade, around the temperature of oil in a big end bearing - the most highly stressed part of an ordinary car engine. Viscosity decreases as temperature increases and at around 100°C, mineral oils start to become very thin and break down. Tests at this temperature are a useful oil strength indicator.

Thank You So much for reading thus far may you be enriched...

https://www.pinterest.com.au/pin/197032552431705570/?lp=true

African plant in black science

What Makes a Plant Magical?
Symbolism and Sacred Herbs in Afro-Surinamese Winti Rituals. Available from: https://www.researchgate.net/publication/263336650_What_Makes_a_Plant_Magical_Symbolism_and_Sacred_Herbs_in_Afro-Surinamese_Winti_Rituals [accessed Jan 02 2019].

Magic had important pragmatic aspects, which were exploited to achieve the aims of humans, dead or alive, spirits, and gods:

Goddess Ausati, where she said **"I am the Nubian and I have descended from heaven" nubia1**, besha Pataikos.
Hearing this the divine Isis said:
I am the Nubian woman
I have come down from heaven
I have come to realize the seed in the body
of every mother's son and every mother's daughter
And cause them to return in good health
For as Horus lives
So shall all live:

Morgan, M (2011) The Ritual Year in Ancient Egypt, Mandrake of Oxford
Pinch, G (1993) Votive Offerings to Hathor, Oxford

Priest Teacher Rabbi LMDumizulu was initiated into primordial practical mysteries. Life "nudged" him on to test and taste through coincidences spiritual forces in Judaism, Christianity, Islam, Yogic and other mystical mental systems. His "out of the box" analysis and conception of life cuts away the divisions created in Politics, Money and Banking, War and Bloodshed, Religion, Bookish Education and Technology. He continues his unending initiation into EXISTENCE and has been outstanding to millions who listen to his **KhamitHiburu Ethics** YouTube channel, reads his healthy channel - Whealthiinc.com website and htpps://www.maarifado.com. He is currently engaged in many non-governmental efforts to rescue all who have realized the subtilty of most religions and culture

PTR LMDumizulu

KhamitHEthics Services..

Contact us; Emails
lmdumizulu@gmail.com/join@maarifado.com.

Website. www.maarifado.com

Made in the USA
Coppell, TX
27 January 2023

11762001R00016